POWWOW
ACTIVITY
BOOK

Jesse & Sandy Hummingbird

Book Publishing Company
Summertown, Tennessee

© 1999 Jesse T. Hummingbird

Cover illustrations by Jesse T. Hummingbird
Cover design by SYTAC Publishing

Printed in the United States of America

Native Voices ☞

Book Publishing Company
PO Box 99
Summertown, TN 38483

931 964 3571

ISBN 1-57067-078-1

Jesse T. Hummingbird, a tribal member of the Cherokee Nation, has illustrated several Native American coloring and activity books. Among his honors are the 1992 Gallup Inter-Tribal Ceremonial poster artist, 1996 Artist of the Year by the Indian Arts and Crafts Association, and 1996 SWAIA Fellowship artist. Jesse currently lives in Bisbee, Arizona.

Native Voices, an imprint of the Book Publishing Company, works with Native American authors and illustrators.

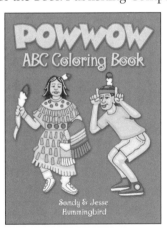

Native American Ledger Art Coloring Book
Jesse & Sandy Hummingbird

Powwow ABC Coloring Book
Jesse & Sandy Hummingbird

Suquamish Coloring Book
Legend of the Basket Ogress
Peg Deam

Yaqui Coloring Book
Stan Padilla

Available from your local bookstore or from
Book Publishing Company • PO Box 99 • Summertown TN • 38483
1-800-695-2241
Each coloring or activity book is $4.95 US or $7.95 Canada. Please enclose $3.50 shipping & handling per book.

The dancer has_____hearts on her costume.

Draw a line from each item to the same item on
the dancer's costume

Draw your own designs on this dancer's shawl.

This dancer has____feathers on his costume.

Color the dancer's hair brown.
Color her shawl red. Color her dress blue.
Color her moccasins yellow.

How many hoops does this dancer have?

Connect the lettered dots and numbered dots to finish this dancer's costume.

Finish the end of the feathers like the one in the dancer's hand.

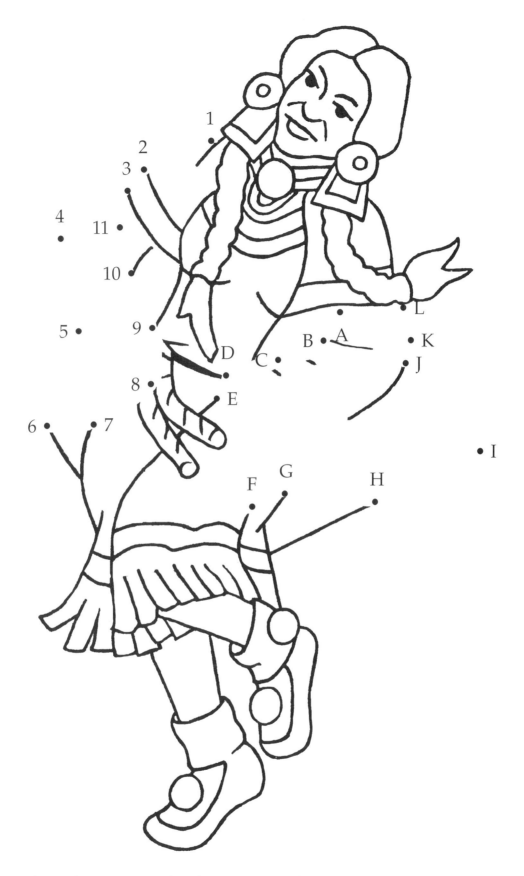

Connect the lettered dots and numbered dots to finish this dancer's shawl.

There are_____dancers in the arena.

There are _____ women and _____ men dancers.

COLOR:
1=brown
2=yellow
3=red
4=blue
5=green
6=black

14

Help this dancer
through the maze to
the dance arbor.

Circle the three dancers that are the same.

Help each of the dancers find the way through the maze to the center ring.

Circle the dancer that has a different costume.

START

FINISH

Help this dancer through the maze to find her
feather.

Circle the 5 items that are different in this dancer's costume.

Circle the 5 items that are different in this dancer's costume.

Circle the two dancers that are exactly alike.

Circle the two dancers that have the same number of hoops.

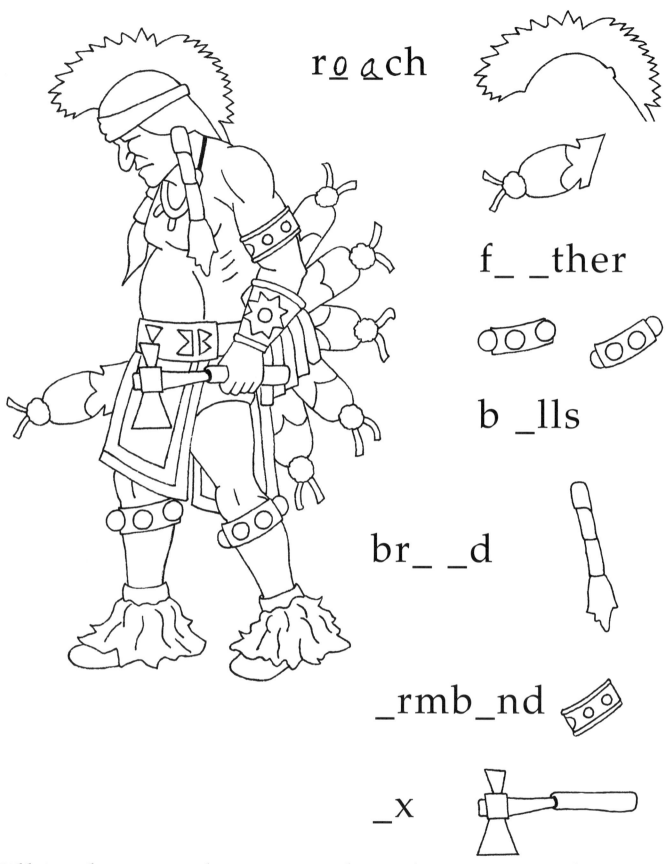

r o̲ a̲ ch

f_ _ther

b _lls

br_ _d

_rmb_nd

_x

Fill in the <u>vowels</u> to complete the names of items in this dancer's costumes.

I	N	N	F	E	A	R	I	N
S	F	E	A	T	H	E	R	O
M	O	C	C	A	S	I	N	T
E	L	K	T	H	H	C	K	H
A	M	L	H	E	A	R	T	S
R	T	A	E	A	W	M	O	C
T	O	C	R	R	L	E	A	N
S	H	E	A	R	R	I	N	G

EARRING

MOCCASIN

FEATHER

HEARTS

SHAWL

NECKLACE

Here are parts of this dancer's costume.
Find and circle the names of each part.

Finish this crossword puzzle with the names from this dancer's costume.

CODE:
1 = A   10 = M
2 = B   11 = N
3 = C   12 = O
4 = D   13 = P
5 = E   14 = R
6 = H   15 = S
7 = I   16 = T
8 = K
9 = L

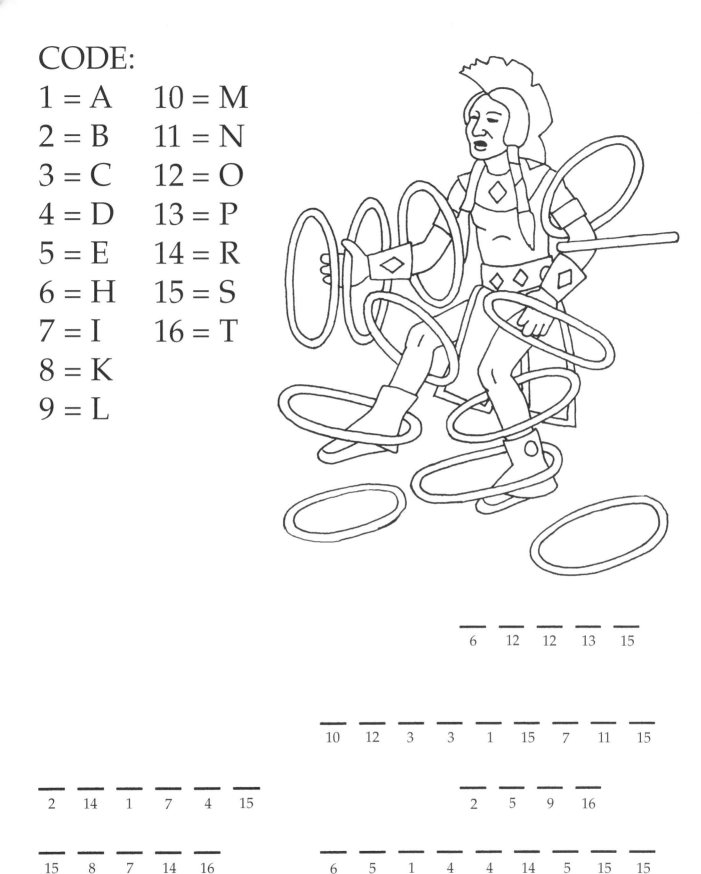

__ __ __ __ __
6   12 12 13 15

__ __ __ __ __ __ __ __ __
10 12 3   3   1   15 7   11 15

__ __ __ __ __ __   __ __ __ __
2   14 1   7   4   15   2   5   9   16

__ __ __ __ __   __ __ __ __ __ __ __ __
15 8   7   14 16   6   5   1   4   4   14 5   15 15

Use the code to name the parts of this
dancer's costume.

The letters in FANCY DANCER can be turned into many words like <u>face</u> and <u>day</u>. How many can you make?

Write your words here:

_____

_____

_____

_____

_____

_____

_____

_____

_____

_____

_____

_____

_____

_____